# This Invisible Beauty

*poems by*

# Tina Egnoski

*Finishing Line Press*
Georgetown, Kentucky

# This Invisible Beauty

Copyright © 2017 by Tina Egnoski
ISBN 978-1-63534-217-8 First Edition
All rights reserved under International and Pan-American Copyright Conventions.
No part of this book may be reproduced in any manner whatsoever without written permission from the publisher, except in the case of brief quotations embodied in critical articles and reviews.

## ACKNOWLEDGMENTS

"The Census Taker" was published in the anthology Forgotten Women: A Tribute in Poetry, edited by Ginny Connors, Grayson Books, 2017

Publisher: Leah Maines

Editor: Christen Kincaid

Cover Art: Lisa Carney

Author Photo: Stacey Doyle

Cover Design: Elizabeth Maines McCleavy

Printed in the USA on acid-free paper.
Order online: www.finishinglinepress.com
also available on amazon.com

Author inquiries and mail orders:
Finishing Line Press
P. O. Box 1626
Georgetown, Kentucky 40324
U. S. A.

# Table of Contents

Scrub Tramp ................................................................... 1
*Los Hermanos* by the Numbers ................................... 2
Make Me a Florida Cracker ........................................... 3
Arachne in the Outhouse .............................................. 4
The Census Taker .......................................................... 5
Mud Dauber: Letter to Maxwell Perkins, I .................. 6
Entomofauna .................................................................. 7
My Life as a Pomegranate ............................................. 8
Indent Heat .................................................................... 9
The Neighbors Have a Say .......................................... 10
Have You Ever: Letter to Maxwell Perkins, II ........... 11
*Garrulus Floridanus*: A Blue Jay Quarrels with
    Everything ............................................................... 12
The Lonely Pecan Tree ................................................ 13
Hellbind ........................................................................ 14
*Os Resectum*: Cold Snap in the Orange Grove ......... 15
The Snake ..................................................................... 16
Every Morning I Walk Orange Lake .......................... 17
The Current Fashions of Cross Creek, 1936: Letter to
    Ernest Hemingway .................................................. 18
Collective Nouns of Central Florida .......................... 19
Our Daily Bread: Folks of the Big Scrub Have a Say ... 20
Late Afternoon Thunderstorm ................................... 21
Novel About a Boy, with Rejoinder: Letter to
    Maxwell Perkins, III ............................................... 22
Flutter-mill ................................................................... 23
Healing Powers of the Egyptian Lotus Blossom ....... 24
This Invisible Beauty ................................................... 25
Notes ............................................................................. 26

*For my sister, Christine*
*for taking me back to Cross Creek, thirty years later*

"It is the Florida of the hammock, the piney-woods, the great silent scrub. This is the Florida, wild and natural, that I'm calling 'the invisible Florida.' Not because it's remote or inaccessible and can't be seen, because there it is, a physical sight plain to anyone."

—Marjorie Kinnan Rawlings
"The Invisible Florida"

Marjorie Kinnan Rawlings moved to Cross Creek, Florida, in November of 1928. She and her husband, Chuck, bought a farmhouse in the middle of a seventy-four-acre citrus orchard. They planned to simplify their lives, earning an income from the sale of fruit, while Marjorie continued her writing career. She fell in love with the pine scrub landscape and with the "Crackers" who lived in the country. At Cross Creek she found her voice. The years between her arrival and the publication of *The Yearling* in 1938 were some of the happiest and most productive of her life.

## Scrub Tramp

Eight-room farmhouse scruffy at the hem.
Porch hip-cocked, unpainted
lady, all armpit and elbow
belly-bowed and angled. Tin roof a bonnet
of rust. There on the crest an eye of patina
catches the sun and winks. She's a flirt shouldered
between lakes Orange and Lochlossa—kindly gentlemen.
*Honey, you won't make a dime
in this orange grove.* Weak-kneed, I paid
thousands to make her mine. Say a sweet prayer
the floorboards don't buckle.

November air smells of thigh
sweat. It cuts the membrane
of my nostril. I'm flimsy.
A tatter
in love. We all bleed
the first time.

## *Los Hermanos* by the Numbers


Infinite bliss—thirty-three hundred orange
trees on seventy-four acres plus eight hundred pecans
tangerine and grapefruit too few
to count
two hundred chickens
with complementary coops
minus the three I found dead
this morning succumbed to the pecking order
two cows two mules one barn two-story
Chuck my one and only
two brothers-in-law
tenant house with a couple of squatters
a couple man and wife
willing to work for board
indoor kitchen faucet only cold but a luxury nonetheless
wood-burning stove iron pot one each
outdoor shower outdoor privy
for all the world to see my business
nothing sacred in this hamlet
veranda veranda veranda so precious I must triple my joy
Rand Remington paper on platen
Lucky Strike lit and ash—millions
and millions of words waiting to be mine.

## Make Me a Florida Cracker

Let quartz sand like vernix swaddle me upon arrival. Let
me suckle on the milk venom of diamondbacks. Let me
teethe on acorn crust. Let me wog-hobble
down to the Ocklawaha.
Christen me in tannic waters.

My bones are sparrow. My fingers
clack-jack twig.

Vowel-feral,
my first words are *twa'n't* and *orter*.
I *goed* and I *mought*—puncture
to the gullet.

Let the blind-love eyes of opossum be my guide. Let
me wrestle and swallow. Let me
wallow in swamp grass bed.

Let me pin the snout of an alligator to my bosom until we are one
one one one mud rapture.
Let Spanish moss sprout from my scalp and make me a hairy crone.

I'm bitten and smitten. I'm home.

**Arachne in the Outhouse**

Intruder, why make your home in this wooden
box like a coffin
upended, foul with body rot? Why only stink-seeking flies
when you can feast on nectar
of beetle? Why shun the sun?

I hear you are a boast
yet hide golden strut-and-trestle—pretty as lattice,
strong as alloy.

Be gone, rival. My superior talents
rule—word-weaver, scene-ripper. This pen
will be my cudgel. This palace my throne.

You mere mortal shall spend your days
out in the world, spinning.

### The Census Taker

> *We entered the River Styx gently. Surely, death itself must come as quietly.* —Marjorie Kinnan Rawlings, *Cross Creek*

On horseback we set forth at dawn. Zelma counts
the living, black and white.
I count vultures. Sparse
shadows, circling. Our mares keep track
of cottonmouth coils
like pie tins half-buried in earth.

Pine prairie swallows hickory hammock—both bellied
by a cypress swamp raw with peat-meat. Horse hocks
part the river lilies. Cattails graze
our shins.

My companion knows every hoof-step
of this backwoods scruff, every local. Tick mark
for turpentine and moonshine stillers, women
with children on knee and at breast. Farmers, square
dancers, story-seers. The migrant and the tenant. Tick,
tick. Squatter, sitter, wagon driver. Tick for outlaws,
tick for in-laws. Hunters, maids, cooks, weavers, fishers, fence
menders, dress menders. Tick for a father
teaching his son to skin a coon. Tick for worshipers, grove
men, gas siphoners, milkers,
nurses, drunkards, sugar cane grinders. Tick, tick,
tick until the pad is blessed with lead.

We turn for home, breach again the river. A heron
wades—white spectral in mourning
hood. We cross and live
to tell tales of the living,
of the living and the alive.

## Mud Dauber: Letter to Maxwell Perkins, I

Dear Max,
I vibrate
solitary wasp
industrious
scrub stories
nested
like pan flutes.

After Milwaukee
and my silly stage
career
after Manhattan
and Rochester
absurd city
life

I'm waist
up in cow muck
knees down
in sandspur nettle.

With spit and grit
I write.

# Entomofauna

May beetles hug the screen, beg
for construction tips: how to build an indoor
privy. Curious brown widow rappels
in for a peek. She spins a tale of sink, tub, toilet
ordered from Sears,
Roebuck. *This I've got to see* declares
the ladybug and brings her friends. Polka-dotted
polka-dots on white-washed walls.
*Sit your fanny right down* advises the palmetto
bug perched on the bowl, antennae atwitter.

Silverfish inhale plaster. Earwigs
circle the pipe funnel. Gluttonous carpenter
ants make a beeline
for chinks in exposed lath.

Mosquitoes want none of it. Their lifeblood
is our blood. Dozens of crickets festoon
the perimeter. Crooners, altruistic
pests, trilling, thrilling—
they serenade the bather.

## My Life as a Pomegranate

Earth sorrow I arrived
lean and feathery, a rooted flout
of bush. Crack-tooth,
ankle-chalk—symbol of prosperity
yet to be. Hostage to climate. Acid
air acid dirt. A stain
of fingerling.

On this fourth spring I'm solid of calyx.
Fibrous, broad-leafed, *so heavy that roof-high slender
boughs are bent to the ground.* Blood ruby
blood red. Carved jewels
in goblet mouth. Wafer crisp
I'm edible
by gods feared
by all beloved.

**Indecent Heat**

Summer invades our makeshift Garden
of Eden. Land sun-scorch
barren. God's sandlot on the boil, eternally
immutable. Through parchment
wall, I smell

air as foul as tobacco
spit and pigsty. In the dooryard
Black-eyed
Susans coerce.

Figure on horseback retreats
in dog-day kick of dust. Chuck
on retreat. Last time
the mare shied, I ate
dirt. Inclement weather bucks
and binds us.

Down at the riverbank
I shed my skin.

## The Neighbors Have a Say

I. Girl in blue dress, barefoot

She weren't no beauty
and I ain't no rangy nit
bit girl neither.

She call me sister and I stole her oranges.
She call me child and I drank her liquor.

When it were all gone I left the bottle neck-tipped
'side the tea tin and ever'body knows that bad luck.

II. Crosby, orchard manager

Her bad luck come in fours: frost, debt, divorce,
illness. Last one laid her up longer 'an I ever seen. Kept her from
garden and grove. From that clack clacky machine.
Don't understand a word she put down but I know
others who know and they's them that like and them that don't.

III. Zelma, friend

Gimp-smile and skunk-stare—I liked
her very much.

## Have You Ever: Letter to Maxwell Perkins, II

Dear Max,
Have you ever tongued
kumquat juice off
your chin? Have you gnawed an orange
pits to pulp to rind?

Have you lounged with chiggers and arisen
thoroughly adored—red and scaly
mite bites under your skin
itching with love?

I suspect not. Men of the three
piece suit and the Fedora
never indulge.
Still I ask: fleas in the broguing
of your wingtips? Hoary boar quick
on your tail?

Have you? Have you.
Ever.

## *Garrulus Floridanus*: A Blue Jay Quarrels with Everything

God gave us voice. He barks, cackles, hisses,
caws, mews, shrieks, natters—insipid gossip—
conjectures, bawls, at times purrs, conciliates,
purely hates kid with bb gun.

Bill and claw
claw to bill
the bird contests a sword
palmetto and wins. Snails and seeds an easy
mark. Tweeze the whiskers off a feral kitten.

He gave us knees, fingers to interlace.
Coincidentally, with pads to bring together.

He gave us *succor, pacify*.

Unschooled squirrel tangles with screecher
destined to lose ear or tail fluff or eye.

He gave *fulminate*, a thing more ominous.

A fair fight requires one to usurp.
Speak first squawks the deity
or retaliate.

## The Lonely Pecan Tree

Persnickety pecan prone to self-pollination.
We—
me and tree—
can alliterate ourselves, can rhyme and
repeat ourselves out of inflorescence.

There is more than one cliché: sweet
meat. Meet me. See, we
carry both inside: bud
and bustle. Desire and its antonym.
Distaste.

We measure meter. At market
we calculate to the ounce
all the words that begin with D.

One critic spoke of dialect. Another
of differences.

In the company of eight hundred
familiars all it takes is humidity,
a stiff breeze.

In spring, catkins snag our arms.
Our eyelashes caper with pollen.

In winter, another November, divorce
papers arrive. I sigh and sign.

## Hellbind

Surrender autumn to machete and viscid
seedpod. Salt tolerant sun muncher
no root
no bulb. Suckers cloak my body
a thousand times a thousand
times.

In science class, I studied the symbiotic
relationship between acacia and twig
ant. Separated, they languish.
My hands are hands
tied. Each incision humiliates
the ardor between climber
and host.

To uproot bone from bark
requires more than hatchet
or lopping shears,
lancet or razor.

### *Os Resectum*: Cold Snap in Orange Grove

Tonight our profits burn. Tepees of cord
wood doppelgang
between rows. Men scurry
kerosene in hand. Kerchief
masked, smoke
choked.

Mercury singles. We see our
breath. We catch our breath
in urns. At dawn—kindling
ash. I snap a twig, brittle
finger to bury
in my palm.

**The Snake**

Braided in just-cut grass—cozy,
persuasive—a lost hair ribbon. City beauty
for a country girl. Ruby and saffron to tie
at my crown. I fist the cord.

It strikes.
Too quick the cheat gone
dissolved into the scalp
of fetterbush.

Coral or scarlet king
one poisonous, one not,
red bands touch yellow
or black in between,
and I can never
remember the difference.

## Every Morning I Walk Orange Lake

Agitate kingfisher, shoal bass, the lip rouged
kiss me kiss me petals of *nymphaeamexicana*—
native Floridian. Silver-plated
minnows and bluegill obey my shadow.

My instinct—to trespass.

In stagnate water, blue herons
curtsy, witness.

## The Current Fashion of Cross Creek, 1936: Letter to Ernest Hemingway

Dear Hem, When you come to Cross Creek—do, do, I beg you, do— don't be surprised to find brassieres bobby-pinned to magnolia trees, yellow-nipped, cups cupped—as appealing to bees as the real deal. My silk stockings have been shredded and strewn, are twine for the nests of whooping cranes. I gifted a cameo brooch to the armadillo, heraldry for her breastplate. You may see clasped and snapped in the teeth of chameleons my handbags or maybe you won't. Clever change-artists: taupe on taupe, mauve on mauve. Panthers prowl in opera-length gloves. Who needs a girdle? *Ursus americanus floridanus* of course, name as bulky as her behemoth backside. She's slimmer and trimmer. When you meet her on the trail, take note. Butter her up. She's one who appreciates a compliment. Nothing for the glad-handing skunk. Same for the rattlesnake. Odious creatures deserve and receive disdain. My white fox stole I ceded to the red fox, cousins in arms. I beseech you, come and delight in my new attire: boots and breeches. No dangles, my only fashion accessories: a .22 and a bird dog I call Mandy.

## Collective Nouns of Central Florida

a pontoon of anhingas

a cloche of opossums

a safety pin of trap-jaw ants

an electric light switch scatter of geckos

a back scratcher of black bears

a step-stone hump of snapping turtles

a double eye-patch of raccoons

an underhand of bobcats

a ligament of Eastern racers

a tea-time tea cup of spring peepers

—these parlor game gifts.

## Our Daily Bread: Folks of the Big Scrub Have a Say

Here we are loyal to Big Yank
chambray Three
Thistles snuff.

Here we spit on a hook and cuss
catfish to take the slimy
bait.

We mail-order. We palmetto
shack marvel.

Here we are vagabond
and derelict
never infallible snobs
peaceable at heart.

Jail our weekend. Wash-bench
all week long. We relish the big bony bay.
We devour the big bony
bull. Corn croquettes on the griddle, swamp
cabbage on the side.  Heifer meek—
give us this day.

## Late Afternoon Thunderstorm

Clockwork—heat and moisture collide. Wind
pole-vaults my spine. I'm electric,
bramble to lip, in awe.

Acorns scutter the roof. I shudder, lightning
blind. Oak and elm, fellow supplicants.
We're swept off our feet.

Over in minutes never too soon.
Mourning doves boast the all clear.

Earth is corpulent, palmetto wet. I lift a limb to expose worm
and weevil larvae, areolas of flesh, lowest life, unfazed.

Will I, Northern transplant, ever abide
this force of nature? This summer ritual?
Will I forever be kudzu, clinging, clawing? Will I be java
plum, thin-skinned, shaken by each thunderclap?

Or one day will I be gaillardia, contented
native, petals licked by rain, nodding
off at the roadside, replete?

### Novel about a Boy, With Rejoinder: Letter to Maxwell Perkins, III

Yes, Max, you may ask about the progress
of the novel. About a boy. Dogs, guns, rivers,
hunts. A novel. Boy's book of the scrub.

> What of bears? In the midst of abundance
> there are always bears.

And bear hunts along the river. Novel about bears.

> And wolves? Mother, father, bear. Wolf.

And mules. There must be mules. Stubborn
and tiresome as words.

> Scrub book about a boy and bears and guns and wolves
> and a fawn.

A fawn? No. Vicious thunderstorms. Storms of my own. Spotted
torment. Procrastination—a river that flows south to north.

> A book then of a boy and a fawn.

Of timber and sugar cane.

> A Florida book, you say. A book I will open. Book
> of the Florida vein. To be opened.

You may ask and I will reply: book about a boy
has me by the throat. And no, no fawns.

**Flutter-mill**

Innocent toy
of twigs and palmetto
strips. Forked,
a-flicker. My heart
laid to rest
in the lick of Juniper Creek.

Hard rain high water. Leaves—
hickory, birch, gumbo
limbo—pinioned.
A dam to stop time
and perpetual motion.

### Healing Powers of the Egyptian Lotus Blossom

The boys wade
lap deep in Lake Orange
gather beauties
to chest
tug.

I forfeit a dime per blossom.

Sun-worshippers, flower and fruit arise
each dawn from muddy swamp
release
reveal tassel of pollen.

From the divan—ancient litter
to carry me through this City of
Recuperation—I hold vigil.

Vased, stems entwine
petals upright
reach for me
compulsory.

I submit, submerge
moon-shy
under their spell.

## This Invisible Beauty

Twilight boat, St. John's River
shoestring current
knotting north
bowing west.

Compass and chart
grow dim on my lap. Futile
companions.

Last clouds cuff the horizon
plumbago bruised knuckles.

Fox-faced moon
impenetrable—
bald and lichened.

Cicada ruckus. Bog
frog bacchanal.
Deafening, delighting.

Pale torsos of cypress
hundreds of living ancients
knob-kneed, armless
ghosts of the shallow.

My oars stir water
enchanted.

**Notes**

Epigraph: From a talk Marjorie Kinnan Rawlings gave at Florida Southern College in 1935.

"*Los Hermano*s by the Numbers": The Rawlings' named the homestead *Los Hermanos* after Chuck's two brothers, who lived nearby and helped them find the property.

"Make Me a Florida Cracker": Rawlings used the term Cracker with great respect to refer to the people who inhabited the big scrub of Florida.

"The Census Taker": In the fall of 1930, Rawlings went with her friend Zelma Casson to take the census of the backwoods of Alachua County. The only way the women could reach many of the remote places was on horseback.

"Mud Dauber": After the publication of "Jacob's Ladder" Rawlings developed a decades-long correspondence and friendship with famed Scribner's editor Maxwell Perkins. He was also the editor for F. Scott Fitzgerald, Ernest Hemingway and Thomas Wolfe.

"Entomafauna": Rawlings published her first story about Florida Cracker life, entitled "Jacob's Ladder," in *Scribner's Magazine* in 1931. With the payment she built an indoor bathroom.

"My Life as a Pomegranate": The line "so heavy that roof-high slender boughs are bent to the ground" is from *Cross Creek*.

"The Lonely Pecan Tree": Rawlings and Chuck divorced in November, 1933, after fourteen difficult years.

"*Os Resectum*": Over the years, Rawlings and her field workers battled a number of severe frosts that damaged the citrus crop. December of 1934 was a winter that rivaled the Big Freeze of 1894-95. In ancient Rome, during the mourning period, a finger was severed from the deceased before cremation. The finger was later buried.

"The Current Fashions of Cross Creek, 1936": In June 1936, Rawlings went with Mrs. Oliver Grinnell to Bimini where she met Ernest Hemingway. They soon began a correspondence and she often urged him to come visit, just as she urged Perkins. Neither one of them ever came to Cross Creek

"Novel about a Boy": Rawlings and Perkins began to correspond about what they called "a book about a boy" or "a boy's book" as early as 1933. She didn't mail him the manuscript until December of 1937. *The Yearling* was published the following year. It became an instant bestseller and won the Pulitzer Prize for the Novel in 1939.

"Flutter-mill": A flutter-mill is a toy waterwheel. In *The Yearling*, the main character, Jody, makes one from two Y-shaped twigs, a cherry tree branch and palm fronds. In the story, the flutter-mill represents Jody's growth from boy to young man.

"Healing Powers of the Egyptian Lotus Blossom": At Cross Creek Rawlings suffered from bouts of bronchitis and malaria. In 1938, after spending time in a Jacksonville hospital, she was diagnosed with chronic diverticulitis and sent home to convalesce. She paid local boys to pick the water lilies and bring them to her.

"This Invisible Beauty": Not long after she moved to Cross Creek, Rawlings took a boat trip on the St. John's River with her friend Dessie Smith Vinson. During the several hundred mile journey, Rawlings delighted in the sights and sounds of this isolated marsh country. She published an account, called "Hyacinth Drift", in *Scribner's Magazine*.

**Tina Egnoski** is a poet and fiction writer. She's the author of two books: *In the Time of the Feast of Flowers* and *Perishables*. Her work has appeared in a number of literary journals and anthologies, including *The Carolina Quarterly, Cimarron Review, The Masters Review, Saw Palm Journal* and *Shoreline*. She's the director of the Ocean State Writing Conference. A Florida native, she currently lives in Rhode Island.

www.ingramcontent.com/pod-product-compliance
Lightning Source LLC
LaVergne TN
LVHW041504070426
835507LV00012B/1319